For Sheila

THE IRISH COTTAGE

PHOTOGRAPHY LIAM BLAKE

TEXT DAVID PRITCHARD

Published in Ireland by Real Ireland Design Limited

First published in 1998 by **Real Ireland Design Limited** ©.
27 Beechwood Close, Boghall Road, Bray, Co. Wicklow, Ireland.
Telephone: (01) 2860799. Fax: (01) 2829962.

Photography Liam Blake ©.
Text David Pritchard.
Book & jacket design Brian Murphy.

Printed in Ireland

British Library Cataloguing in Publication Data.
A catalogue record for this book is available from the British
Library

ISBN 0946887349

INTRODUCTION.

The words 'Irish Cottage' evoke a very special kind of house, a white-walled thatched haven in a peaceful and green countryside or beside the wild Atlantic waves. Outside of her cities and towns, Ireland is still a country of cottages of one type or another, although in the last fifty years more modern houses have appeared on the rural landscape. Nobody can relate the full history of Irish cottages, for by definition they were the dwellings of the poor and built to last only a few short lifetimes. Often those rare cottages which play some small part in Irish history make their appearance only to be destroyed, as in the cabins of the Glenveagh evictees, abandoned after their owners were forced out of Ireland by the landlord John Adair.

For each cottage which has connections to the mainstream of Irish culture and history, there are thousands whose inhabitants have gone unrecorded. Yet the rich peasant traditions of those who dwelt in cottages has been a consistent thread running through the fabric of Irish life. Whilst the ownership of the land passed from one race of masters to the next, it was tended and tilled by peasants whose ancestors had belonged to the nameless peoples who settled Ireland in prehistoric times. The traditional cottage reflects this legacy, incorporating the most ancient features with newer ideas learnt from Norman, Scottish or English conquerors.

This book is a celebration of the Irish cottage and an examination of its evolution and place in Irish society. Liam Blake's photographs, taken over the last twenty years, form an invaluable pictorial record of the traditional cottage in the closing decades of the 20th. century. In many images his artist's eye captures the unique aesthetic qualities of limewashed thatched cottages and their relationship to the stark western landscape. Others are less poetic and encapsule the irony or humor of the cottage in decline, yet nevertheless add to our understanding of the importance of the vernacular dwelling in an age where it has been superceded by the bungalow and modern house.

The text which accompanies these photographs is divided into three sections. The first part explains the historical background and architecture of Irish cottages and farmhouses, both the traditional thatched type and later versions introduced into Ireland by the Landlord class and public bodies seeking to house the poor. The second section deals with the design and folklore attached to the longhouse cottage and its predecessor the byre-cottage, the most typical forms of traditional dwelling. Lastly, the legacy of the Irish cottage is discussed in the context of the decline of the clachan settlement and the emergence of one owner farms and the modern bungalow.

It is to be hoped that this book will encourage the appreciation and preservation of traditional cottages and farmhouses. Like the castle or tower-house, the stone rural cottage has become obsolete and been replaced by more comfortable - if not more beautiful - dwellings. Yet thousands still remain, some still inhabited whilst others are abandoned and falling into decay. Traditional cottages are an integral element of the Irish landscape, adding interest and scale to the countryside. Sympathetic rebuilding and restoration helps maintain an important resource which is of the greatest value to Ireland's architectural heritage.

THE HISTORY AND ARCHITECTURE OF THE IRISH COTTAGE.

The earliest people who arrived on the shores of Ireland about 10,000 years ago were nomadic Stone Age hunters who had no need of permanent dwellings. They lived in small settlements of temporary wood and hide shelters, which could be broken down and moved on to the next camping site. But with the advent of farming in Ireland around 4000 B.C. the building of more permanent dwellings began. Archaeologists have excavated a number of ancient farmhouses, most notably at Ballyglass (Mayo), Lough Gur (Limerick) and Ballynagilly (Tyrone), with the result that it is possible to reconstruct their appearance. In many ways these prehistoric dwellings have remarkable similarities with their counterparts in more recent centuries. All had thatched roofs and prominent hearths, features which are still typical of the traditional Irish cottage, whilst the house at Ballyglass had the rectangular ground plan and gabled roof ends found in the 'long house' cottages of Scotland and the west of Ireland. Other excavated prehistoric dwellings are circular or oval, a design which might have fallen into disuse over the last 100 years but was before then

Beehive hut, Slea Head, Co. Kerry.

Two storey farmhouse beside Staigue Fort, Ring of Kerry.

Thatching in progress, Co. Sligo.

quite common in remoter areas of Ireland.

The most important distinction between prehistoric Irish farmhouses and their more recent counterparts was in the materials used. Wood was the main component in their construction, reflecting the heavy forestation of Ireland in those times. Over the last 150 years the stone cottage has become so much the norm that we forget that it is a comparatively recent innovation, replacing other

building materials which were prevalent in the dwellings of the Irish countryside until after 1800. Where stone was used for dwellings in earlier times it was mainly utilized for low foundation walls on which clay and thatch houses were raised, or for the clocháns - or beehive houses - erected in the treeless coastal areas of the west of Ireland. This is not to suggest that there was no tradition of stone working in Ireland, since Neolithic tombs indicate that from the earliest times stone constructions were built

Longhouse cottage, the Mourne Mountains, Co. Down.

using sophisticated corbelling techniques. However, stone seems to have been favoured for more important buildings like tombs and stone circles in prehistoric times and churches, castles and tower-houses in the Middle Ages.
Except in some western areas the majority of the ordinary population lived in houses of cheaper and less durable materials than stone, which have disappeared - except from folk memory - in the rural building boom of the last couple of centuries.

The most important building material for peasant dwellings throughout most of Ireland's history has probably been simple mud. This is one of the most basic of all building materials and in Irish tradition is associated with poverty and the lowest rung of the social ladder. Yet in ancient times great civilizations like the Indus culture of present day Pakistan and Bronze Age China were based on the mud building. In Ireland the mud-walled house was usually of 'clay and wattle' construction, raised on a plinth of

Small Cottage, Ferns, Co. Wexford.

stones, roofed with thatch and then limewashed for added protection. Carefully built clay and wattle houses were probably more comfortable than stone dwellings, since they retained their warmth better in winter. However, they fell prey to the harsh Irish weather more quickly and did not have the durability of stone cottages.

Clay and wattle cottages were used by the lower classes of Irish rural society in most regions until well after the Potato Famine. The census of 1841, a few years before the Famine started, estimated that almost 40% of the entire population were living in one room rural mud cabins, a harsh testament to the poverty and overpopulation of huge areas of the country. Yet despite its bad name in Irish tradition, mud was used in regions where stone was unavailable to build quite substantial houses for wealthier farmers. It was also the favoured medium for the cottages of the poor in cities and towns, until replaced by stone and

Tin roof cottage, Co. Meath.

brick artisan cottages in the Georgian and Victorian eras.

A not dissimilar material used in most districts of Ireland was the turf sod or 'scraw'. Scraw houses were possibly easier to construct, since their walls did not have to be allowed to dry in layers like clay and wattle houses. Sometimes built as a lean-to against a bank or ditch for convenience, the turf cabin probably offered a remarkably dry and comfortable dwelling from a free and readily available

source which had exceptional insulating properties.

Despite the prevalence of mud and sod houses and cabins over most of Ireland, in some areas there was an ancient tradition of cottage building in stone. Visitors to remote and treeless Achill island in the years before the Famine described the dwellings of the population as circular or oval thatched huts of rough boulders, built without mortar and having no windows or chimneys and very

Cottage gable, Kilmore Quay, Co. Wexford.

small doorways. Similarly, some early photographs from Donegal and other western areas show clachans - or hamlets- of primitive gable-ended rectangular cabins and outhouses which appear to be the prototype of the more sophisticated 'traditional' thatched two-roomed cottage and longhouse dwellings associated with the Irish countryside.

The movement of the rural population into the variety of more permanent and better built cottages and farmhouses which now decorate the Irish countryside began in the 18th. century, gained momentum after the Famine of the 1840's and continues to this day. It was initially encouraged around 1700 by improving economic conditions and a long period of peace after the cataclysmic wars of the 16th. and 17th. centuries. In the decades after the Great Famine of the 1840's the decline in population and the emergence of larger smallholdings in many areas made it possible for more of the rural population to afford to build stone dwellings. The last and most important impetus to replacing sod and clay and wattle cottages came with the Land Acts of the 1880's and 1890's, which allowed huge numbers of tenants throughout Ireland to buy their farms and become landowners.

The surviving thatched roofs on vernacular Irish cottages and farmhouses reflect regionalized styles, which have been handed down from earlier centuries. Until the 19th. century thatch was the universal covering used for most ordinary rural buildings, including tower houses, churches, schools and industrial buildings as well as cottages. Slate roofs are a comparatively recent introduction to rural Ireland, whilst tiles have only been used to cover cottages in the last 50 years or so. From the Victorian era onwards the common replacement for thatch was the 'corrugated' roof of sheet steel, an effective and cheap material which deserves more respect than it receives from modern planners and architects. Painted and rust free corrugated sheet roofs were almost as attractive a roofing material on cottages as thatch and much easier to maintain.

Thatched roofs were traditionally made from wheat straws, although rye, oats and barley straws were also popular. In Ulster, where linen manufacturing was very important, flax straw was commonly used, giving the distinctive silver grey sheen on the thatch of many northern cottages. In older times reeds, rushes

Liscannor slate roofed cottage, Doolin, Co. Clare.

and even heather were common thatching materials in areas where grain straws were unavailable or difficult to obtain. Whilst there were several methods of thatching, the two which were generally preferred reflected the main types of traditional cottage developed in Ireland.

The two-room hip-roofed cottage with a central chimney was predominant over most of Ireland outside of the western seaboard and some of the remoter inland areas. This form of cottage had no pointed gable end and its thatch rose from the four sides of the house at roof level. In most hipped roof dwellings thatching was by means of scollops (willow or hazel rods), which pinned down the thatch. Along the western coasts, on the other hand, cottages had stone gables to the apex of the roof on their narrower ends and thatch was tied down by ropes which were weighted with heavy rocks or pegged to the cottage walls. Pegged thatch gave roofs a particularly attractive rounded appearance, still seen

Tin roofed cottage, near Lough Dan, Co. Wicklow.

Two storey cottage on estuary, North Donegal.

occasionally in old cottages in Donegal, Mayo and Galway. The chimney would be placed on a gable end rather than against the dividing wall as was normal in hipped cottages.

The common explanation for the variation in the design of cottages between the west and east is that hipped cottages were introduced into Ireland by the Anglo-Normans in the Middle Ages, whilst the roped thatch gabled cottage is an older and more genuine Irish type.

However, since hipped cottages are found in areas where the Normans did not penetrate, it is as likely that the differing methods of construction were caused by the use of stone for cottage walls in the gale swept west and clay and flimsier walling materials in other areas where the weather was milder.

A distinction must be drawn between the typical peasant cottage and the more sophisticated dwellings erected by wealthier farmers of the 18th., 19th. and

Extended cottage, Ballyness Bay, Co. Donegal.

early 20th. centuries. Broadly speaking there are two basic types of rural farmhouse, common throughout Ireland. The first is the longhouse, where the building is only one room deep and two or more rooms lead into one another, and a separate shed for animals is attached to one end. This is the most traditional form of farmhouse and possibly has very ancient roots. Certainly many of the folk beliefs associated with the type appear to be very ancient. The oldest surviving longhouses date from about 1700, but it is obvious that they are a more developed version of the primitive one- and two-room rectangular cabins which Irish peasants shared with their cattle in winter.

The fully evolved longhouse dwelling was far more comfortable than its rougher predecessor, the byre cottage. It was roomier, with a separate shed for animals and a chimney instead of an open hearth. Its windows, on the other hand, remained comparatively small in

Two storey cottage, Dingle Peninsula, Co. Kerry.

number and size, partly because glass was still a luxury but also because houses were taxed by window size until the 1850's. Generally longhouse farms were of very solid construction and whitewashed to enhance their appearance. Longhouses - with either gabled or hipped roofs - are the most common type of traditional dwelling found in the modern countryside today, although all too often slate and tiled roofs have replaced the original thatch or corrugated covering.

Longhouse dwellers who required more living space sometimes extended their houses upwards. The simplest way of doing this was to place a loft room at one or both ends lit by a gable window. However, from about 1900 onwards the thatch in some long houses (and smaller cottages) was replaced with slates or tin and an upper floor with two or more bedrooms installed. These tiny dormer rooms were usually reached through a staircase in the kitchen and lit only by

Single and two storey cottages, St. Finian's Bay, Co. Kerry.

The Swiss cottage, Cahir, Co. Tipperary.

small gable end windows. Cottages with reduced upper floors - a 'house and a half' as some call them - are found all over Ireland.

In other cases, especially where the thatch was hipped, another solution to the problem of space was to strip off the roof and heighten the walls. Many of the two-storey farmhouses of West Cork are raised longhouses and still have walk through ground floors. For the most part these extensions were carried out after

1900, when thatched roofs were usually replaced with slate or iron. However, the comparatively small number of thatched two-storey hipped or gabled long houses are amongst the finest Irish vernacular dwellings.

The second main type of farmhouse is the two-storey hall plan house, which is a simplified version of the large and medium Georgian estate houses introduced into Ireland from about 1700 onwards. 'Hall' farmhouses may be distinguished from heightened longhouses by their full size upper floor and internal plan, which has a hall inside the front door with rooms leading off and a staircase. They might be called 'Five Window' farmhouses since their facades are usually quite severe in the classic style, with two evenly spaced pairs of upper and lower windows and a fifth window above the central front door. Many of the smaller Georgian farmhouses of the 18th. and early 19th. century have a generally similar floor plan, which undoubtedly served as a model for later versions. From the Victorian era to the 1950's - when the bungalow became popular - sturdy lime-washed or painted hall farmhouses with slated hip-roofs were the typical dwelling house on larger and more prosperous farms.

The rural dwelling most strongly associated with Ireland, the thatched and lime-washed longhouse cottage, will be dealt with in more detail in the next section. Yet they are only one of an astounding diversity of cottage types found in Ireland. Privately built cottages and farmhouses are supplemented by a bewildering array of other small dwellings raised by a variety of employers and institutions for their workers or the rural poor. Most of these cottages were not in the traditional or post-Georgian style favoured in Irish vernacular architecture, but were influenced by contemporary English ideas about cottage design. At the same time stone cottages and farmhouses were replacing mud cabins in Ireland, there was a strong movement in England to provide better housing for the rural poor. 18th. century books like John Wood's 'Plans for Cottages' (1781) offered a variety of stylish and quaint small houses for labourers and estate workers. Similar books of the following century like J.C. Loudons 'Encyclopaedia of Cottage Design' (1841) and John Vincent's 'Country Cottages' (1861) were particularly influential in Ireland, and Victorian cottages in Medieval, Tudor and other romantic styles outnumber traditional houses in some districts.

These 'alien' cottage types were introduced to Ireland via a number of sources. Amongst the oldest are ornamental gate lodges and decorative cottages, the earliest of which belong to the 18th. century and pre-date most surviving traditional cottages. Since gate lodges often mimic the style of the great houses whose entrances they protect, they can take the appearance of miniature castles, colonnaded 'Grecian' hous-

Cottages, Adare, Co. Limerick.

es, Georgian rotundas or one of a dozen other styles or mixture of styles. Perhaps the most visually pleasing are those in the quite severe classical style of the 18th. century, with their balanced facades and fine Georgian windows.

Gate lodges and the other decorative houses and cottages on the demesnes of the Anglo-Irish landlords often sacrificed comfort for an elegant external appearance and tended to be small and pokey behind their outward opulence. But they were real houses which were used to accommodate servants and their families. In this they differed from the 'fantasy' cottage, a building more akin to the folly, which was meant to amuse and entertain rather than act as a genuine dwelling. The most famous example of this type is the 'cottage orné', developed in 18th. century France for aristocrats who wanted to play at being peasants. The Swiss Cottage in Cahir (Tipperary) is amongst the most spectacular surviving cottage orné in Europe and full of the

Lighthouse cottages, the Hook, Co. Wexford.

Canal cottage at Clashganna, Co. Carlow.

quaint rustic detail which make these bizarre buildings so compelling. It dates from the early 1800's and was built to the design of John Nash to embellish the estate of the Earls of Glengall.

Far more important than gate lodges and decorative cottages are the dwellings erected in the model villages associated with some great estates. The classic medieval English village, with its ancient parish church, manor house and quaint old houses simply does not exist in Ireland. With one or two exceptions the only domestic Irish dwellings surviving from before 1650 are medieval tower-houses and the fortified mansions of the Jacobean era. Most of manorial villages introduced into the Irish countryside by the Anglo-Normans had been destroyed in the later Middle Ages and survived only as settlements of flimsy clay and wattle cabins huddled around some tower-house or abbey. Along the west coast the equivalent of the village was the clachan, a small cluster of randomly sited cottages belonging to an extended family group. In heavily settled areas clachans might form almost a ribbon development, but whilst they functioned as communities they lacked the amenities which distinguishes real villages.

Estate villages were an artificial solution to this dearth of 'proper' villages, introduced by socially conscious landlords in the 18th. and 19th. century. They replaced the earlier clay and wattle settlements of their tenants with well built and often picturesque cottages and provided churches, parish halls, schools and shops. The finest model villages, like Tyrrellspass (Westmeath) and Adare (Limerick), are amongst the most attractive communities in rural Ireland, offering a variety of one- or two-storey cottages and distinctive features like horse-shoe doored forges. Originally built to house the workers of a single estate, they have become successful in their own right and now service the surrounding areas. Other communities which started their lives as estate villages have grown into substantial market towns, for instance Mitchelstown (Cork).

Industrial villages and cottages parallel their counterparts in the great agricultural estates. Sion Mills (Tyrone) and a number of other villages originated in the 18th. and 19th. centuries as housing for the employees of enterprises like mills, mines and quarries. Industrial villages were usually quite small and lacked the exuberant architectural

Cottage outbuildings, Bloody Foreland, Co. Donegal.

panache of many estate villages, opting for rather formal terraces of simple if well built cottages. Quite a number did not survive the demise of the industries which sustained them and have now disappeared or been reduced to ruins. Curiously, the idea of the industrial village was revived in the 1940's and 50's when Bord na Mona established new villages for its workers at Coill Dubh (Kildare) and Clontusket (Roscommon).

On a smaller scale the expanding transport and maritime services of the 18th. and 19th. centuries dotted the Irish landscape with small clusters of workers cottages in the vicinity of canals, railways, coastguard stations and lighthouses. For the most part these were simple rectangular stone or brick dwellings with slate roofs and fairly basic accommodation within, although they were of markedly superior building quality to the average rural farmhouse and cottage. Today many railway and canal cottages are in private hands and have merged

Colourful cottage, near Waterford city.

into the general category of country cottage.

A last and extremely important source for Ireland's stock of rural cottages are public bodies like the Congested Districts Board, Land Commission and County Councils, who have provided free and subsidized housing from the late 19th. century up to the present. Their cottages were intended to house farm labourers and craftsmen who could not afford to build their own houses. As part of the policy of giving these landless tenants some opportunity to grow their own food, most 'public body' cottages stood on an acre of land, so that terraced examples often have very long and narrow gardens by modern standards. The contribution of public housing to improving the lives of the rural poor was immense, since for many it offered the only chance of escaping from unhealthy and substandard accommodation.

Public body cottages may be seen

Coastal cottage, Malin More, Co. Donegal.

Cottage with extended outbuildings, Fanad, Co. Donegal.

throughout the Irish countryside in a variety of styles and configurations, usually in small groups of up to a dozen units. The earlier types are normally terraced or paired rows of simple one-storey cottages, detached hipped-roofed bungalow-like dwellings with brick trimmings, or paired two-storey houses with the upstairs lit by a single projecting dormer or a gable window. Later Council cottages - i.e. from the 1920's onwards - sometimes come in quite exotic styles which reflect developments in the design of artisan houses in Britain and Europe. Rows of A frame cottages with high peaked roofs - like those in Laragh Co. Wicklow - or square cottages with 'Georgian' windows and pyramidical tiled roofs with a chimney at the apex - add a new architectural dimension to country villages.

The categories of cottage mentioned above contribute an important diversity to the architectural heritage of the Irish countryside. However, in a sense they

Extended two storey cottage, Ballycrovane harbour, West Cork.

Traditional cottage, Clogher Head, Co. Louth.

are a parallel development to the vast numbers of privately built cottages and farmhouses which form the bulk of Ireland's rural dwellings. These range in size from large and quite impressive two- or even three-storey classical houses on large properties, to simple one-room thatched fisherman's or labourer's cottages. Most are complemented by ancillary buildings ranging from a simple lean-to shed to a full farm complex with stores, barns and milking-houses.

The distribution of these farms and other associated rural buildings like churches, pubs and shops is governed by the nature of the landscape and the type and scale of farming in any particular region. The rich flat plains of Meath, for example, provide a very different environment to the rocky valleys of the Wicklow mountains or Donegal highlands. The archaic communal clachan survived in mountainous and boggy areas throughout Ireland until the verge of the modern era, but elsewhere it seems to have been

Two storey cottage, Waterville bay, Co. Kerry.

replaced since medieval times by individual farms whose labour was carried out by a floating population of labourers and craftsmen. Other regional differences in building styles have been caused by the influx of settlers from Scotland, Germany and England into parts of Ulster and Munster.

Nevertheless, the vernacular cottages and farmhouses of rural Ireland have many common features that suggest the movement into more permanent stone dwellings began around the same time throughout the countryside. Even today, when the emergence of the bungalow has swamped and depleted Ireland's stock of traditional buildings, enough older cottages and farmhouses remain in use to make Irish country roads amongst the most consistently picturesque in Europe.

THE TRADITIONAL LONGHOUSE COTTAGE

The archetypal Irish cottage - if such a thing exists - must be the longhouse, a type of dwelling that probably has roots going long into the past. Existing longhouse cottages are rarely older than two hundred years but there can be little

doubt that they are heirs to a much older tradition. Some of the folklore beliefs associated with this type of cottage seem to have originated in pagan times, whilst the distribution of longhouses through the British Isles seems to be associated with areas belonging to the 'Celtic rim' of Western Europe. The Irish traditional cottage is an important member of a family of related domestic dwellings which are heirs to one of the oldest architectural heritages in Western Europe.

The closest equivalent to the Irish longhouse may be found in the highlands of Scotland, which until the 17th. century shared its language and culture with its neighbours across the narrow straits dividing the Western Isles from Ulster. The thatched stone cottage and clachan settlement were as prevalent in the Scottish highlands as they were on the west coast of Ireland and Scottish Gaels and Irish Gaels had a common stock of folk beliefs attached to their longhouses. In Scotland, however, the Highland clearances had an even more devastating effect than the Famine in Ireland and the building of traditional cottages petered out more quickly.

In southern Scotland and the Border

Cottage gable, Inishbofin Island, Co. Galway.

Cottage door, Roundwood, Co. Wicklow.

counties of England, longhouses were popular until the end of the 19th. century, although most surviving examples are slated rather than thatched. One unusual early form of longhouse was the 16th. century 'bastle house' - a fortified dwelling which had a basement for cattle on the ground floor and a walk through upper floor with protected windows reached by a external staircase on a gable end. The Cumberland longhouse - a type common in the mountainous Lake District - had its barns built beneath the same roof ridge as its living accommodation, an arrangement much favoured in Ireland.

Further south the Welsh traditional cottage resembled the simplest Irish longhouse cottage in having just two rooms and a hearth. Many are thatched, as indeed is common in similar cottages found even in the south east of England. The Cornish longhouse bears even more resemblance to those of Ireland, being built of unhewn rocks without mortar and having a thatched roof or sometimes one of flat stones. The oldest Cornish longhouses are believed to date back to about 1450, but the style generally died out about 1800 and was replaced by more conventional hall farmhouses.

To some extent the distribution of stone longhouses in the British Isles is influenced geographical factors. Whether on Dartmoor, in Argyle or in Donegal they are found in areas where wood is scarce and weather conditions too harsh for mud or clay houses to be a viable alternative. However the similarity between longhouses in these varying regions suggests they share a common descent from a type of dwelling much older than any surviving examples. The clachan pattern of settlement has parallels in excavated Stone Age villages like Skara Brae in the Orkney islands of Scotland, where huts are linked together to form a small contiguous hamlet. The long one-room rectangular byre-house from which the longhouses of the British Isles derived must have evolved by the early centuries of the Christian era, since after about a.d.500 the links between Ireland and the Celtic influenced areas of Cornwall, Wales, northern Britain and south-west Scotland were weakened or broken.

Traditional Irish cottages and clachans are perhaps best viewed as the last vestiges of a way of life that in prehistoric times was the norm in many of the countries of the Atlantic seaboard of Europe. The distribution over the British Isles of

Farm cottages, St. Finian's bay, Co. Kerry.

prehistoric megalithic tombs, stone circles and cashels resembles that of longhouse cottages, suggesting a long history of contact and interchange between the regions that bordered the Irish and Celtic seas. In a very real sense the Gaelic smallholders and fishermen who inhabited the cottage clusters of the Atlantic coasts of Ireland were heirs to a process of learning that had began thousands of years earlier when the first Stone Age migrants followed the retreating Ice Age into the British Isles.

There seems little doubt that longhouse cottages had extremely ancient origins, perhaps incorporating even Stone Age features and beliefs in their architecture and folklore. In older times, for example, it was very common for longhouse cottages to have built-in stone benches beside the hearth and stone 'keeping' shelves in the wall to the left and right of the fire. Similar arrangements are found in the Neolithic huts of Skara Brae (Orkney Islands), which were situated

Winter view of cottage, Doolin, Co. Clare.

within the area of longhouse distribution in the British Isles. Connected to this is the evidence that in the cottages of Skara Brae woman stored their possessions (and presumably sat) to the left of the fire and men to the right. The same tradition persisted both in northern Scotland and on the west coast of Ireland into the present century.

The true ancestor of the longhouse is probably the 'byre-house', a single-room rectangular cottage which had one end reserved for its human inhabitants and the other for their animals. This 'pig in the kitchen' lifestyle was much commented on and derided by English observers in the 19th. century and became a standard joke about the Irish peasant. 'At one of th'ends he keeps his cows, At th'other end he keeps his spouse' as William Moffat wrote of Highland byre houses in 1724. However it was actually the usual practice of smallholders throughout Europe for thousands of years, especially those who concentrated on tending cattle rather than growing wheat or other grains.

Partly the byre-house was a viable dwelling because the practice of 'booleying' - or moving cattle from upper to lower pastures - meant that animals had only to be housed in the winter months. In spring, cattle were brought up to their summer grazing and kept there until late in the year. Their herdsmen - mainly the boys and young men of the community - were housed in primitive round, oval or rectangular huts of turf and stone, the booley houses whose foundations may still be seen in some higher fields in the west. For much of the year byre-houses were inhabited only by their owners and his family.

The longhouse cottage was a more comfortable extension of the simple byre-house, which increased in popularity after the decline of booleying and the emergence of compact one family farms from 1700 onwards. Initially, perhaps, a shed was built onto the end of the one room cottage to house cattle or a second more private room added behind the wall containing the hearth. Once the cattle were housed separately in a shed at the end, the builders of longhouses could add as many rooms as they liked to the side of the house opposite the hearth. The extended byre-cottage, with its attached cattle shed, formed a long, low range, hence the name longhouse.

Longhouses varied in width from about ten feet to twenty feet, but were never

Farm cottages, Beara, Co. Cork.

Cottage Bolus Head, Co. Kerry.

Tin roofed cottage, at the foot of Benwisken, Co. Sligo.

more than one room deep, although in some northern and eastern areas a screen wall was placed behind the door to form a simple hall. Their length depended on the number and size of rooms in the dwelling, which might vary from as few as two rooms to as many as five. The classic Irish type of longhouse has three rooms, each leading into the other, and a cowshed with a separate entrance attached at the furthest end from the fireplace. The central room served as a kitchen, with the hearth and chimney (if the house had one) usually placed on the wall to the left of the entrance. The main bedroom was to the right of the kitchen, whilst the third room was situated on the far side of the hearth wall.

This third room, the room 'behind the fire' or 'to the west' had a particular sig nificance, since it was associated with death. It was not usually in everyday use, but rather kept as a 'best' room in which mementoes of dead parents and

Half-door cottage, Inish More, the Aran Islands, Co. Galway.

other relatives were kept. If old or sick people were in the house they would sleep 'behind the fire' and if anybody in the house died their bodies were laid out in this room during the wake. Many superstitions surrounded the back room of longhouse cottages. In Mayo, for instance, it was considered dangerous to extend a house beyond the back room, since death would inevitably follow within the year. The association between death and the west room, which faced the setting sun, may be the vestige of very ancient beliefs about ghosts and death. Certainly Stone Age farmhouses in Ireland and elsewhere are often found beneath megalithic tombs or barrows, suggesting they were used as the burial sites of their owners.

The cottage was entered through a door leading into the kitchen, which was the main living room. In the north and west of Ireland longhouses had two entrances, placed opposite each other on either side if the kitchen. These allowed cows

Two storey cottage, Glengarriff, Co. Cork.

Two storey thatched cottage, Mooncoin, Co. Kilkenny.

to be brought in and out of the kitchen for milking in bad weather and by closing one or the other doors fire-smoke could be dispersed regardless of the prevailing winds. The favourite type of entrance door in traditional cottages was the half-door, which permitted the lower part to remain closed whilst the open part let in air and light. The introduction of chimneys and milking sheds made a second door superfluous and in many cottages with this arrangement it was later closed off or converted into an extra window.

A number of folk traditions were attached to the back door. In some areas new born or newly bought animals were brought through the house by its double doors for luck. A stranger was not allowed to leave via the back door (generally used only when the wind was blowing 'the wrong way') in case he take the luck of the house with him. Corpses were taken out by the back door and all the front doors in the clachan closed as the funeral cortege passed by. Other traditional superstitions concerning death suggest beliefs that long predated the Christian era.. People were put on the cottage floor to die or if they died in a bed it was immediately burnt. It is recorded that often a plate containing

tobacco, salt or turf was placed on the corpse's chest, presumably in the belief this might help preserve the body. Even odder are stories of food and pairs of shoes being left in coffins to help the deceased on his journey to the next world, practices totally at odds with Christian ideas about the afterlife.

The half-door helped compensate for the poor quality of cottage windows, which were often little more than crude holes in the wall.. Windows - one per room - were placed on the side of the house away from the prevailing winds. They were extremely small, partly because they were generally unglazed but also because in the first half of the 19th. century - when many stone cottages were built to replace earlier dwellings - houses were taxed by the size of their windows. Instead of glass, cottage windows were closed off with wattle frames, dried hides and sheepskins or even sheep's placenta. The opening was wider inside the thick cottage wall than outside, rather in the fashion of castle or tower-house windows.

Before chimneys were introduced into cottages, the hearth was left open and smoke allowed to disperse through the thatch, windows and doors. This made

Coastal cottage, Achill Island, Co. Mayo.

early cottages extremely uncomfortable and their stools and other furniture were kept low to allow those using them to sit below the thick clouds of smoke billowing in the upper part of the house Despite its negative aspects, allowing smoke to dissipate through the long-house had some very beneficial effects. It kept vermin out of the thatch, but above all distributed warmth throughout the whole building and kept it dry in a way which chimneys could not. In fact it might be argued that one of the reasons traditional cottages sometimes feel so cold and damp today is that the open, smoking hearth has been replaced by chimneys which draw off much of the heat of their fires.

To take advantage of the heat rising to the top of the thatch, some longhouses were provided with half or double lofts with floors of clay or matted reeds. Stone cottages with such lofts often had tiny windows high up in the gable to provide light. These lofts served to store

Colourful cottage near Mallow, Co. Cork.

Cottage window, near Rosslare, Co. Wexford.

clothes or items that could be damaged by damp, because the smoke hovering beneath the eaves of the house kept them bone dry. Traditional longhouses with an open hearth were unsuited for an upstairs or attic, since a full ceiling would have made the ground floor unbearably smoky.

The hearth was the core of the longhouse cottage, around which its economic and social life were centred. Peat, the natural cooking fuel of the Irish countryside, burns much quicker than coal or wood, so that fires were traditionally placed at floor level rather than on a raised grate, to avoid draughts. In prehistoric and medieval Ireland, hearths were inevitably placed in the middle of the floor, but by the 18th. century they were normally situated along the dividing kitchen wall in the longhouse or on a gable end in the one-room byre house. Old style cottage floors were made of packed clay, which was hard wearing but could not take the heat of a fire, so the base of the hearth was a large stone or cobbled area.

Chimney breasts were a comparatively late introduction to the Irish cottage, judging from their style perhaps first appearing in the 1600's as copies of those in planter's houses. In the south and east of Ireland they sometimes took the form of wattle canopies, which were raised above the fireplace on a wooden platform which served as a rough mantelpiece. Over the rest of the country they were generally made of limewashed clay and reached down to ground level to surround the hearth. Chimney tops were squat and without pots, although it was not uncommon for them to be thatched in keeping with the cottage roof.

In more recent times the use of coal - a less combustible and slower burning fuel - led to several innovations in the technology of the hearth. Sometimes the fire was raised by means of a grate but in many cases the draught was increased by installing a built-in bellows with a tube leading into the floor of the fire. In some very sophisticated hearths a pit was placed beneath a floor grate into which ashes could fall and be removed without disturbing the fire.

Cooking on the hearth involved the use of a variety of tools. Perhaps the most important was the crane and pot hangar, which allowed pots to be hung over the fire. The crane was simply an L shaped wood or iron contraption which project-

Small cottage near Askeaton, Co. Limerick.

ed an arm over the fire. It was usually placed on the left of the fire (traditionally the woman's side) and could often be pivoted out of the fireplace for convenience. Pot hangars were commonly made of iron and were suspended from the overhanging arm to hold cooking pots.

A variety of pots and pans were found in traditional kitchens. Undoubtedly the most notable was the three legged cauldron of cast-iron, with its two brackets beneath the rim for attaching pot handles. This particular type of pot is vary ancient and may be traced back - although without its triple legs - to very similarly shaped Neolithic earthenware pots. The ancestors of the cast iron pot include the beautiful bronze cauldrons of the Bronze and Iron ages seen in Ireland's National Museum and the round bellied leather and clay pots used in medieval households. The cauldron cooking pot has taken an important role in Irish mythology and folklore - and indeed has a sacred role in other cultures as diverse as West Africa and China.

One cooking aid not found in traditional Irish cottages was an oven, although in the 20th. century the kitchen range has often remedied this deficiency. Meat was cooked over an open fire, in pots or during earlier ages on a spit or stretched hide. Wheaten yeast bread has never been a native Irish food, and the common form of bread was a flat loaf or cake made from oats, barley or potatoes. These were baked on flat griddle irons which were hung above the fire or on toasting racks propped up in front of the hearth. The most primitive form of rack was a forked stick or flat stone, but the more sophisticated wrought iron version - the bread or oatcake toaster - was often decorated with folk art motifs such as spirals.

The domestic and agricultural crafts associated with traditional Irish life were usually carried out in the kitchen. Spinning was a particularly ancient skill, as shown by the discovery of whorls in Neolithic settlements. The spinning wheel developed from the basic spindle and whorl was found in many longhouses, either in the large version common in Connemara and Munster or the smaller treadle wheel of Ulster which was originally developed to spin linen yarn. Clothes like socks and waistcoats were knitted at home - although the pullover was a late19th. century introduction brought to Ireland by sailors from the Channel Islands - hence the use of the terms 'Jersey' and 'Gansey' (Guernsey).

Weaving was almost as old as spinning, the first looms having appeared in Ireland during the late Bronze Age. Until curtailed by an Act of the English Parliament in 1699, there was a flourishing export trade in woven materials, most of it produced in mills and workshops. After the decline in the woollen trade following this Act, most weaving was done by weavers working in their cottages, which were traditionally built higher than normal to provide room for their looms. In the 1890's - in an attempt to boost the woollen industry - the Congested Districts Board introduced the much faster 'fly shuttle' loom used in linen mills to weaving areas in the West of Ireland, thus laying the foundations for todays highly successful Donegal and Connemara tweed industries.

Whilst intended only for domestic use,

Small cottage, Connemara, Co. Galway.

Dan O' Hara's cottage, Near Clifden, Co. Galway.

woven baskets, mats and sieves of straw made attractive and useful utensils and were found in most cottages. Where straw was not available, reeds, heather, or hazel twigs served as natural alternatives. As with most rural crafts, basket making had a long history in Ireland, probably dating back to the introduction of cereal crops before 4000 B.C.

Much of the work done in cottage kitchens was concerned with processing milk products. Butter making was an important and laborious task consigned to the women of the house. In earlier times butter churns and milk measures were made of wood, but during the 18th. century they began to be replaced by metal and ceramic jugs and pitchers. In wealthy homes these utensils were made of silver and treated as prized possessions. In the east and south of Ireland, butter was made from the cream of the milk only, whilst in the poorer west and north the whole of the milk was used.

Colourful two storey cottage in Eyeries village, Westcork.

Row of fishing cottages, Portmagee, Co. Kerry.

A final range of domestic chores related to maintaining fishing implements, both for freshwater and sea use. These included lines, hooks and forked spears for inland and shore use and drift and ring nets for those few remote communities which practised the dying art of deepwater fishing in the 19th. century. Most of these tools for fishing aids were made locally or at home, using natural fibres like hemp and horsehair for nets and lines. Worn out nets were often used in the stormy north and west to help tie down thatched roofs. Fishing has certainly been practiced in Ireland for at least 10,000 years and the traditional west coast curragh, with its wooden frame and hide skin, probably has a long history. An even older type was the small oval curragh in use on the river Boyne until about fifty years ago. The materials used in this boat, which is made from a wicker basket covered with oxhide, were exactly those available to the Neolithic farmers who raised the

Two storey thatched cottage, Enniskillen, Co. Fermanagh.

tombs of Knowth and Newgrange, suggesting that the Boyne curragh might have been in use for over 5000 years.

The busy economic activity of the cottage kitchen was balanced by a rich social life. Storytelling and conversation were centred on the hearth and their own homes were the only meeting places for the inhabitants of most clachans, resulting in many superstitions and folktales concerning the dangers of giving or refusing hospitality to strangers

and mysterious guests. Singing was undoubtedly an ancient and important part of the heritage of the clachan and with the introduction of instruments like the fiddle, flute and pipes in the 18th. and 19th. centuries the foundations of Irish traditional music were established.

Sleeping accommodation varied according to the wealth and number of inhabitants in a cottage. In the poorest one-room cabins there were no beds and the family slept 'in stradogue' or on the

Cottage door with porthole, near Dungloe, Co. Donegal.

Modern farmhouse cottage, Slea Head, Co. Kerry.

Large two storey thatched cottage, Blackwater, Co. Wexford.

'thorough-bed'. This simply meant that they lay naked on bundles of rushes, huddled together beneath a communal plaid or blanket with their feet to the fire. A more sophisticated arrangement was to have a wooden or stone bench which could be used as a seat by day and a bed by night. In Donegal and Connemara cottages often had an outshot, an alcove projecting out from the cottage wall to hold a bed. Outshots may have originated in Scandinavia, since they appear to have been brought to Ireland via the northern and western islands of Scotland settled by the Norse in the Viking period.

Outshot beds allowed some privacy, but were a poor substitute for a separate sleeping room for the cottier and his wife. Children in one-bedroom longhouses continued to sleep together in the kitchen by the fire, whilst a second hearth and chimney were installed on the gable end to heat the bedroom. In three-room longhouses a hearth might be placed on the wall of the back room behind the main kitchen fireplace, so it could share the chimney.

The furnishings of traditional cottages were generally home-made and functional rather than elegant. Indeed, until the end of the 19th. century good quality furniture was found only in the houses of the wealthiest Irish farmers. The most common item was the wooden stool, made low so it could avoid the smoke rising from the fire and three-legged to give stability on uneven clay floors. Low tables, a rough dresser and a rope mattress bed might complete the range of furniture in most Irish cottages. Even outside of the treeless Atlantic coasts, beds and other cottage furniture were usually made of bog wood or imported softwoods, since native Irish oak has been hard to come by after the destruction of her forests in the 17th. century.

The traditional longhouse cottage was not merely a home, but the sum of a way of life that had been evolving for many thousands of years. On the west coast the economy of cottage dwellers was a mixture of gathering, fishing, crop tending and pastoralism which allowed continuity of life in a harsh and very difficult environment. Elsewhere in Ireland until the end of the medieval period, agriculture was heavily dependent on cattle rearing, with some cereal production. The introduction of the potato after 1600 caused a major increase in population because it allowed large numbers of people to be sustained on small areas of land. Richer parts of Ireland benefitted from improved agricultural methods in the 18th. and 19th. centuries which led to greater wealth and finer houses for some tenant farmers, although these were a minority. Elsewhere, other smallholders divided their lands into smaller parcels to provide plots for their children, thus increasing the numbers of the rural poor and reducing living standards.

Eventually this led to the end of the longhouse tradition of cottage building. The devastation caused by the Famine and the huge tide of emigration to the United States changed the face of rural Ireland. A reduced population encouraged larger, more amalgamated farms which could support a family in some comfort. This trend - which had begun long before 1800 and is still in progress today - led to the two-storey farmhouses and attached complexes of farm buildings which today predominate over much of Leinster, Ulster and the eastern portions of Munster.

Ornate cottage, the Phoenix Park, Dublin city.

Cottage window near Enniskillen, Co. Fermanagh.

In the far west of Ireland the decline of the traditional Irish cottage took much longer. Most remaining clachan settlements were broken up by 1940 and replaced by rationalized farms, but many of their inhabitants continued living in their longhouses and cottages. It was only in the 1950's, with the arrival of the block built bungalow, that the move into houses with modern amenities began for many families. This process was accelerated with the increase in farm income and the expansion of the Irish tourism industry during the 1960's. Thousands of old stone dwellings were abandoned for more comfortable and warmer single or two-storey houses which often stand beside or near to the cottages they replaced. Nevertheless, although modernized and often with tiles replacing thatch and corrugated roofs, many longhouse and two-room traditional cottages remain in use today.

THE LEGACY OF THE
IRISH COTTAGE

As we have seen in the last section, an important aspect of the Irish cottage is the continuity of an ancient architectural and folklore heritage. The inhabitants of the Atlantic coasts of Ireland and Scotland developed their unique culture out of the mainstream and were closer to the prehistoric roots of Western Europe than other societies. Nevertheless the life of the Irish countryside was not static overall and changing conditions were reflected in the development of differing types of dwelling, especially following the Anglo-Norman conquest of Ireland after 1169. Some, such as castles and tower-houses, had little influence on cottage or farmhouse development. Others - the houses of Scottish planters in Ulster or the smaller Georgian country houses for instance - undoubtedly exerted strong influences on the architecture of rural Ireland.

To a large extent the decline of the traditional cottage in the 19th. century was a response to historical and social impulses rather than architectural tastes or trends. The process of rehousing the rural poor which began in Victorian times was caused by a combination of genuine charitable impulses and a policy of governing the Irish through kindness rather than repression. Whilst the cottages erected by landlords, the Congested Districts Board and Councils might seem small and cramped to modern eyes, they were a vast improvement on the temporary clay and sod cabins which they replaced. They are in effect one of the visible fruits of the appeasement of the Irish peasantry after a long period of vicious oppression.

The results of outside pressures on the rural economy may be traced in the decline of clachan settlements. Before they were broken up and replaced by isolated single farmsteads after the Famine, clachans were the basic communal unit in many western districts. Clusters of farmsteads, with stone walled fields divided into individually owned strips and tiny 'lazy bed' plots around the cottages, had probably been a feature of the Irish countryside since the earliest times. Yet, although clachans provided food and shelter for thousands of years, their associations in the Irish psyche are predominantly negative. Partly this is a result of the 'bad press' received from English travellers who visited them during the 18th. and 19th. century and recorded their poverty and squalor. Yet many of these still shocking accounts, written when the clachan system was in decay, are tinged with racial prejudice and the inability to see the worth of shared communal values in the life of clachan dwellers.

In a very real sense the clachan was not brought low by 'progress', but rather by the introduction of the potato as the main Irish staple food crop in the 1600's, which caused the fragmentation of its landholdings into ludicrously small pieces. The harmful effects of the potato on the fragile economy of the clachan system may be seen in the problems faced by the Congested Districts Board, founded in 1891 to encourage the development of overpopulated western regions and amalgamate their scattered landholdings into cohesive farms. When, for instance, the Board attempted to rationalize the clachan of Rathlackan (Mayo) in 1918, it was inhabited by 56 families. Their holdings were divided into no less than 1,500 different plots, the smallest only about a dozen square yards in area. On average each farm in the settlement held 27 separate pieces of land, divided between open strips on commonly held single fields and small walled infield enclosures adjacent to the cottages. It took 25 years to disperse this clachan and consolidate it into fairly compact farms for 32 families.

Rathlackan was no different than hundreds of other settlements throughout the west of Ireland, indeed many were bigger and had even more complex divisions of land. By modern times the clachan system had become an archaic leftover, too primitive for modern farming techniques. Yet, for all their failings clachans were the source of an irreplaceable treasure trove of folklore and legend. The Irish language survived longer in the western areas of clachan distribution, harbouring much of her best literature in the writers of the remote and now abandoned Blasket Islands. It is not coincidental that most the few remaining Irish speaking areas are the in districts of Galway, Kerry and Donegal where clachans lingered longest.

The rediscovery of the Gaelic culture still nurtured in the cottages of the west by Irish artists and writers in the later 19th. century provided much of the inspiration for the 'Irish Literary Renaissance'. W. B. Yeats and lesser known poets like Joseph Campbell introduced themes and images from the folklore and life of the West of Ireland to the outside world. The plays

Cat on cottage window, West Cork.

Derelict cottage near Mallow, Co. Cork.

of the Abbey Theatre, notably those by Lady Gregory and J.M. Synge, offered characters to challenge the thuggish or comic stereotypes of the rural Irishman created by Punch and other English illustrated magazines. The English of plays like 'Riders to the Sea' is particularly interesting, since it is so obviously the transitional dialect of rural Irish people who have recently changed over from speaking Gaelic. Much of the poetry of language in Synge's plays comes from the use of translated Irish images and modes of speech and is yet another testament to the richness of life in the clachan settlements.

Irish artists began using the western districts for subjects from the 1820's onwards. The early works of the watercolourist Frederick William Burton, for instance, include the remarkable 'Aran Fisherman's Drowned Child' (1841), a depiction of islanders mourning a dead child in his family's cottage. Around 1900 a new generation of Irish painters

New and old cottages near Portmarnock, Co. Dublin.

discovered the west of Ireland. The ink and watercolour drawings of Jack Yeats depicted life on the Aran Islands, whilst the landscapes of Connemara and Achill Island by Paul Henry offered a potent vision of little white cottages against dark mountains and looming, cloudy skies. Henry and his contemporaries initiated a tradition of painting which remains strong to this day, when there are hundreds of artists living and working in the West of Ireland.

The wake, one of the great mainstays of the social life of Ireland and an important element in Irish literature, undoubtedly originated in the cottage settlements of an earlier age. The attitude towards death in traditional Irish society was particularly moving, since it gave open expression to both the need to mourn the dead and to emphasize the joy of life in the face of death. The grief of the community was expressed through the keen, the eerie wailing of female relatives and neighbours that until recently

Pádraig Pearse's cottage, Connemara.

distinguished funerals along the western seaboard. The keen was superbly described by Synge in 1906, after witnessing a funeral on the Aran Islands.

'The grief of the keen is no personal complaint for the death of one woman over eighty years, but seems to contain the passionate rage that lurks in the heart of every native of the island. In this cry of pain the inner consciousness of the people seems to lay itself bare for an instant and to reveal the mood of beings who feel their isolation in the face of the universe that wars on them with winds and seas. They are usually silent, but in the presence of death all outward show of indifference or patience is forgotten, and they shriek with pitiable despair before the horror of the fate to which they are all doomed.

Before they covered the coffin an old man kneeled down beside the grave and repeated a simple prayer for the dead. There was an irony in these words of atonement and Catholic belief spoken by

Cottage at dusk, the Aran Islands.

voices that were still hoarse with the cries of pagan desperation.'

The wake might be viewed as the other half of the ritual of death, an affirmation of life involving informal games and amusements, often of a highly erotic nature. Mourners at wakes put aside their normal behaviour for displays of indecency which resembled pagan fertility rites. According to the 18th. century writer Maria Edgeworth 'more matches were made at funerals than at weddings'.

The entertainment at wakes included mock weddings and beddings and games like 'Bout', 'Making the Ship' and 'Turning the Spit' which involved nudity and sexual intercourse. Several of the games mocked the clergy and in others participants dressed in animal skins, a clearly pre-Christian rite. In time these sexual and sacrilegious aspects of the wake were suppressed by the Church, but it remains an important social occasion where drunken and wild behaviour is more acceptable than on other occa-

Cottage, Slea Head, Co. Kerry.

Cottage near Mount Brandon, Dingle Peninsula, Co. Kerry.

Traditional two storey farm cottage, Beara, West Cork.

Longhouse cottage, North Kerry.

sions.

The beneficial folklore and linguistic heritages of the cottage's contribution must be balanced against the grinding poverty and destitution which are the darker aspect of its legacy. The decades leading up to the Great Famine and its dire aftermath were catastrophic to the rural psyche. Potato blight was not unknown before the 1840's and there had been shortages of food and disease in 1739, 1821, 1831 and 1835/1839. Yet throughout the early decades of the 19th. century, other sources of food were being abandoned. The fishing industry of Achill island for example, which had reached its peak in the decade after 1800, was irreparably damaged by the decline of the Atlantic herring shoals. The islanders turned their backs on fishing as a livelihood and by the time of the Famine there were barely a half dozen curraghs left on the island. The people of Achill island died of starvation by the hundred because they had no means of

catching the abundant fish in the surrounding waters.

The Famine was the beginning of the
end of the old way of life. Scots-Irish
emigrants from Ulster had been flowing
into the American Colonies throughout
the 18th. century, introducing the longhouse and the sod cabin into the
Appalachians and parts of the South as
the tide of settlement moved west. From
the 1840's onwards they were joined by
vast numbers of Catholic emigrants as
the rural and urban poor fled the strick-
en Irish economy. The decline in population caused by the Famine and emigration led to many clachans being deserted in the decades after 1850.

One such lost village was Slievemore on
Achill, which at one time was amongst
the largest settlements on the island.
The group of clachans strung along the
mountainside at one time held over a
hundred simple rectangular stone byre-
cottages with archaic features like stone
bed-slabs and wall storage. At some
date after the Famine the surviving
inhabitants moved out of their sturdy little houses (they had walls over two feet
thick) and started a new settlement at
Duart, which had previously been their
summer booleying pasture. The

clachans on Slievemore mountain were
left deserted and allowed to slowly disin-
tegrate.

The experience of Achill Island after the
Great Famine typifies the changes in
many remote Irish communities in the
later 1800's and the early decades of this
century. Between 1841 and 1851 the
population declined by about 900, or
20% of the total number of islanders. In
the years immediately after the Famine
emigration peaked, then tailed off as life
returned to some semblance of normali-
ty. In the early 1880's, during a period of
economic collapse and political turmoil
in rural Ireland, emigration increased
again. In 1882 a fund was set up by
James Hack Tuke to help promote migration from the West of Ireland. In 1883
alone 44 Achill islanders left for the
United States on assisted passages and
an even larger number departed with the
help of the Tuke fund the following year.

Whilst these clearances helped reduce
the population, they robbed Achill and
other western areas of much of their
able-bodied population. The 'American
Wake', a gathering to say goodbye to the
young migrants leaving their communities by the dozen, was an annual and
heartbreaking event along the west

False fronted cottages, Ardgroom, Co. Cork.

coast. Many of the families left behind in the poverty stricken rural districts became dependent on the money sent back from relatives in America, hastening the end of the self-sufficient clachan system.

Alongside permanent migration, seasonal expeditions to Britain to work on the potato harvest became a feature of life in many parts of Mayo and Donegal. In the early 1900's as many as 2000 men and women were leaving Achill alone annually to work for the summer in the 'tatie squads' of southern Scotland. Despite the appalling working conditions and unhygienic accommodation experienced by labourers, the practice of seasonal migration continued into quite recent times. One of its few positive benefits was that it kept at least some young people from permanent emigration and brought much needed revenue into the economically depressed western districts.

Thatched cottage, Co. Donegal.

Eviction was another darker aspect of cottage life in the decades after the Famine. Tenants on small plots of less than £4 value who fell behind with rents could expect little mercy from landlords, who became liable for their unpaid rates. Often it made better economic sense for landlords to buy tickets to America for defaulting tenants and demolish their cabins so nobody else could live in them. Some landlords rationalized their estates by wholesale evictions, emptying thousands of acres of the bulk of their inhabitants. Events like those at Glenveagh (Donegal), where John Adair cruelly evicted dozens of families after the murder of his estate agent, left an indelible stain on the memories of thousands of migrant families. Many of the old photographs of evictions in the Lawrence Collection are posed, yet the contrast of stern bailiffs, policemen and battering rams with glum evicted cottiers and their furniture strongly evokes the nightmarish quality of the experience.

Cottage door, Virginia, Co. Cavan.

Cottage at Croagh Patrick Mountain, Co. Mayo.

Cottage near Listowel, Co. Kerry.

One victim of eviction had a profound effect on the history of the rural landscape. Michael Davitt's family were evicted from their cottage at Straide (Mayo) in 1852 and forced to make their living in the cotton mills of Lancashire. The young Davitt became a revolutionary and was a major figure in the Fenian Brotherhood before being imprisoned by the British in 1870. Upon his release in 1877 he went to the United States and with the help of Irish Americans like John Devoy began agitating for land reform in Ireland. The successful campaign of Davitt's Land League for the 'three F's' of fair rent, fixity of tenure and free sale led eventually to the breaking up of the landlord system and turned tenants into independent farmers.

The success of Davitt's agitation for land reform led to improved living conditions and housing for many farming families. The gradual growth of prosperity in rural Ireland during the 20th. century acceler-

Two storey cottage, Dunmore East, Co. Waterford.

ated after 1960, triggering off a new wave of building which brought modern and non-traditional types of houses to the countryside in large numbers. The 'bungalow', a Hindi word appropriated by the English language to describe modern one-storey houses, has become the standard small size rural dwelling, whilst larger farmhouses have been erected in an array of styles, many which take little account of their surroundings. The hinterlands of cities like Galway have become planner's nightmare as ribbon developments of large and small suburban houses creep into the countryside and the counties around Dublin are experiencing an inrush of commuters who travel daily to the capital.

There is little way of knowing to what extent the negative experiences of poverty and repression have affected the descendants of the 19th. century cottiers. Certainly on one level the appearance of some modern farmhouses suggests a turning away from the old styles

Two storey cottage near Ballinskelligs, Co. Kerry.

and patterns of thought. The sprawling ranch-type houses and haciendas found in wealthy agricultural districts reflect an indifference to tradition, an urgent need to throw off the shackles of the past. On the other hand the majority of modern rural houses are comparatively modest block-built dormer or one storey dwellings, which impinge on the landscape only by their newness. With their tiled roofs and white walls they are an acceptable and pragmatic continuation of the legacy of dwellings for single

owner farms established over the last century.

It is all to easy to criticize rural people for abandoning their old cottages from the comfort of a modern suburban house or apartment. But in reality the standards of hygiene and comfort in many old cottages are hopelessly outdated. Few were built with toilets or bathrooms and their rough stone construction and poor foundations leave many liable to severe dampness problems. Thatched roofs may be 'quaint', but compared to more modern materials they are expensive to install and have short life spans. Given the expense of renewing and expanding their rackety - if picturesque - cottages, many households with limited budgets find it easier to build a new home. Similarly, flat-roofed extensions to the back of existing cottages may appear ugly and out of context, yet they are the cheapest and simplest means of adding much needed space to cramped two- or three- room dwellings.

The modern block built bungalow is part of a new wave of settlement and change sweeping the Irish countryside, the fourth perhaps since the Middle Ages. The first began with the Anglo-Norman invasion, which brought the manorial system with its structured villages and towns. Although much of this colony was swept away in the 14th. and 15th. centuries its influence remained strong over much of the eastern half of the country. The second period of change started around 1700 with the establishment of the Anglo-Irish agricultural estates. The 18th. century saw attempts to establish rural based industries and improve communications and transport systems, whilst much of the Irish countryside owes its present appearance to changes in farming during this period.

The third great era of change followed the Land Acts of the late 19th. century, which established a huge new class of independent farmers. With the help of the Congested Districts Board and later the Land Commission the outmoded clachan system was dismantled in the remote areas where it survived and the rural poor given decent accommodation. The last 100 years have seen great improvements in the accommodation and life-style of rural Ireland, including such important innovations as electricity and the telephone. The opportunities afforded by the entry of Ireland into the European Community have led to more specialized and efficient farming, resulting in increased prosperity for many.

The most recent revolution in rural Ireland has been brought about by improvements in transport and communications. Since the Famine the flow of population has been out of the countryside, through emigration abroad and to Dublin and the other cities. Poverty and unemployment have overcome all efforts to defeat them in many rural districts and the number of those involved in agricultural activities continues to fall. Even today Ireland's population is barely

Gate cottage near Ashford, Co. Wicklow.

half what it was in the years before the Famine and the greatest losses have been in the countryside

The last twenty years, however, have seen the beginnings of a move back to the countryside. Tourism has brought millions of visitors to the West of Ireland, reviving impoverished economies and bringing jobs and livelihoods to thousands. Simultaneously there has been a growth in reverse immigration as outsiders come to settle or buy holiday homes in areas like West Cork or Connemara. For many city dwellers better roads and the motor car have made it possible to commute into their workplaces from country homes. This has led to the influx of a large number of new inhabitants into the rural hinterlands of cities like Dublin, Galway and Cork. Given the trend towards working from home, this penetration of the Irish countryside seems bound to continue for many years. The fax machine and the modem may well turn out to be the tools

Gate cottage, Killarney National Park, Co. Kerry.

of the most potent new wave of settlement since the first Neolithic farmers drove their oxen onto the shores of Ireland.

The opening up of large areas of rural Ireland countryside has had some beneficial effects on vernacular housing. In counties like Wicklow and Galway, which have strong traditions of cottage building, many derelicts have been bought up by outsiders and restored and modernized to the highest standards. Architects have begun to design houses which take account of vernacular tradition and fit into the rural landscape rather than obtrude on it. Finally new houses made in natural alternatives like stone rather than modern building materials are becoming more common.

One particularly heartening trend has been the reappearance of the wooden cottage. In prehistoric times wood was probably the primary building medium in Ireland, notwithstanding our damp cli-

One roomed thatched cottage, Ballyconneely, Co. Galway.

mate. Timber framed and wooden walled buildings were probably fairly common until the destruction of the Irish oak forests, but in recent centuries wood has disappeared as a prime material for permanent domestic dwellings. The last decade, however, has seen wooden houses return to the Irish countryside. Some are of Scandinavian and Finnish log construction, whilst others are built from planks or wooden panels. The natural properties of wood and modern preservation techniques make the

wooden cottage a warm and durable alternative to concrete or stone. As importantly perhaps, wood offers an attractive variant to the standard modern bungalows and houses springing up along rural roads.

The wooden house brings the story of the traditional Irish cottage back to its prehistoric roots. Few types of building have such a long and respectable history or have held so tenaciously to their environment. Perhaps the key to understand-

Council cottage, Ballinaclash, Co. Wicklow.

ing the continuing attraction of these primitive and uncomfortable dwellings lies in the feeling their inhabitants shared an insight into the human condition that modern man has forgotten. Whilst they sometimes held poverty and despair, rural cottages were part of a gentler way of life, where neighbours supported each other and nobody was alone in times of sorrow and need. In the hurlyburly of modern urban society, so full of personal isolation, tension and aggression, the white thatched cottage on a peaceful mountainside evokes a lost innocence, the memory of a world where a little was enough and satisfaction could be found in humble things.

Colourful cottage and outbuildings, North Donegal.

Group of cottages near Dun Aengus the Aran Islands.

Reconstruction of a Clachan, Glencolumbkille Folkvillage, Co. Donegal.

Books in this series:

The Irish Pub
The Irish Cottage
The Irish Castle & Abbey
Ireland

Liam Blake was born in Dublin, he is the author of several photographic books and has exhibited his photographs in solo and group exhibitions. He has won many awards including best photographic book 1985.

David Pritchard was educated at Trinity College, Dublin and now lives in South Wicklow. His published works include books on Irish postage stamps, an illustrated anthology of Irish poetry and a number of books for Real Ireland Design.